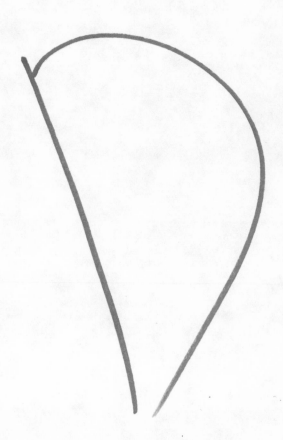

Young Abigail Adams

Young Abigail Adams

by Francene Sabin

illustrated by Yoshi Miyake

Troll Associates

Library of Congress Cataloging-in-Publication Data

Sabin, Francene.
  Young Abigail Adams / by Francene Sabin; illustrated by Yoshi
Miyake.
     p.   cm.
  Summary: Describes the young life of Abigail Smith, who married
John Adams and ultimately became a First Lady.
  ISBN 0-8167-2503-9 (lib. bdg.)   ISBN 0-8167-2504-7 (pbk.)
  1. Adams, Abigail, 1744-1818—Juvenile literature. 2. Presidents—
United States—Wives—Biography—Juvenile literature. [1. Adams,
Abigail, 1744-1818. 2. First ladies.] I. Miyake, Yoshi, ill.
II. Title.
E322.1.A38S22 1992
973.4'4'092—dc20
[B]   91-17112

Young Abigail Adams

The early-morning sunshine made golden
squares on the wooden floor. Little Abigail Smith
looked at the squares of light and smiled. They
made her think of her favorite game, Scotch-
hoppers. That was what hopscotch was called in
colonial times. Seven-year-old Abigail was good
at the game. Better than her sister, Mary, who
was nine. And lots better than her brother,
William. But he was only five, so that didn't
really count.

Abigail wanted to rush outside and draw the Scotch-hoppers design in the dirt. Playing was so much more fun than doing chores. But it was a family rule—chores first. After that came study time. Then—and only then—was it all right for the children to play.

The little girl finished sweeping the dining room. Every day she swept the parlor, dining room, front hall, and the staircase. When it didn't rain or snow, Abigail also swept the front steps and the walk. Sweeping was one of her daily chores.

The sound of a horse's hooves drew Abigail to the window. She hoped it meant Papa was home. William Smith was the minister of the North Parish Congregational Church of Weymouth, Massachusetts. Almost every day he visited a different church member at home. Reverend Smith was very serious about his work.

"We are put on this earth to do right, Nabby," he often told Abigail. "To do our duty, to help others, to listen to them with care and love. And we must respect the rights and ideas of every person. You are still too young to understand. But you will learn that these rules make for true happiness."

As Reverend Smith got off his horse, Abigail hurried to greet him. He leaned down and stroked her hair. "How is my fine young daughter this morning?" he asked.

"I'm very well, Papa. I have finished all my chores," Abigail said, pulling her father by the hand toward the house. "Please, could we go into the library and read now?"

Reverend Smith smiled. "I fear I saw some leaves on the front steps. I know you take pleasure in your lessons. But you must finish your work. And I must rest a bit. I have just spent a long night visiting the ailing Widow Lawrence. Have patience, child. That is another of life's lessons."

Abigail was disappointed. Patience, duty, rules...
these were harder to learn than arithmetic and
spelling. Like all children, Abigail loved to play.
But children in colonial America had little time
for play. As soon as they were able to understand
what they were told, they were expected to do
their share of the work.

In many ways, eighteenth-century children were treated as small adults. That included the way they were dressed. Men and boys in well-off families wore knee breeches, waistcoats, and ruffled shirts. Their hair was powdered and curled and sometimes covered by wigs. Boys were small copies of their fathers.

Little girls like Abigail wore clothing just like their mothers'. They wore low-necked dresses, thin scarves over their shoulders, long stockings, and flat, buckled shoes. In the winter, girls put on shawls or capes to go outside. Colonial women and girls did not wear coats. Only men and boys did.

Children weren't only supposed to look like adults. They were also expected to act grown-up. Farm children toiled in the fields next to their parents. The children of merchants worked in the family stores. As a minister's daughter, Abigail had special duties, too. She had to sit still and pay close attention in church. Sunday services lasted from morning till night. The only break came in the middle of the day, when everyone went home for dinner. All the children of Weymouth attended church and had to behave properly. But Reverend Smith's children had to be the best-behaved of all. They knew they were expected to set an example.

Abigail's mother, Elizabeth, was the perfect eighteenth-century minister's wife. She was a fine housekeeper, an intelligent woman, and a leader in the Weymouth community. Mrs. Smith was a quiet woman who did many things well. She made sure her house was spotless, that meals were tasty, and that her husband and children were well taken care of.

14

The truly hard housework and gardening was done by servants. But there was no chore that Mrs. Smith did not know how to do herself. "It is important for you to know everything about your household," Mrs. Smith told her daughters. "We cannot know what life will demand of us. So we must be prepared to do whatever is necessary. If you are fortunate, you will have others to direct. But you still must know how to direct them."

16

For these reasons, Mrs. Smith made sure her daughters learned to do many things. When they were still quite young, Mary and Abigail learned to spin thread, to weave on a loom, to sew, to dip candles, to cook, and to bake. Abigail obeyed her mother and became good at these tasks. But the reasons for doing the work didn't make sense to her. "I know I shall never need to dip candles," Abigail told Mary. "Nor shall I ever look at a sheep in her warm dress and think that I must take it off her and put it on my back." Then both girls giggled as they continued to spin thread the way their mother had instructed them to.

But when Abigail was a woman, she remembered her mother's lessons with pleasure. As Abigail Adams, she needed to have many skills. John Adams, her husband, was a member of the Continental Congress, a group of men who helped unite the American colonies against England. John was away from home for many months at a time. From the first days of their marriage in 1764, John was often away attending to his law practice and to politics. With John gone so much, Abigail had to run their home on her own.

Before the war with England, Abigail used her homemaking knowledge to instruct her servants and to buy goods wisely. But the coming of war changed everything. The American Revolution brought hard times to Massachusetts. Some people even went hungry.

The British Army was taking a large share of the food grown in the colonies. The American troops, under General Washington, also needed supplies of food. And because many of the farmers had gone to war, there were few workers to plant and harvest crops.

Abigail Adams faced the same problems as everyone else in providing for her family. And she was able to meet them well. Almost single-handedly, Abigail ran the family farm and took care of her five children: Abigail, John Quincy, Susanna, Charles, and Thomas. At first Abigail had one farm-hand. But he left in the middle of haying season to join the Continental Army.

Even so, Abigail brought in the hay, corn, flax, and vegetables. She fed the livestock, and made butter and cheese. She also spun, wove, and sewed clothing for herself and the children.

None of this would have been possible without her mother's teachings. Every time Abigail remembered how annoyed she was at Mama's lessons, she laughed. And when her own children groaned at doing chores, Abigail heard herself as a little girl, and she laughed some more.

Abigail Adams told her children, "These are hard times. Brave soldiers are fighting for our independence. Your papa is away, working to get help from other countries so we can win our freedom. *Our* part in the war is to be truly independent, to take care of ourselves. So we must provide for ourselves in every way. There will be time for pleasure when the war is won."

Of course, when Abigail was a child there was no thought of war with England. The English king was the colonists' king, and the colonists felt a strong tie to their mother country. And the more the colonists were like their cousins across the Atlantic Ocean, the better they felt.

Colonial Americans copied the English in many ways. If English gentlemen changed the style of their wigs, colonial gentlemen did the same. When English ladies favored a new dress style, colonial ladies rushed to copy them. The latest songs sung in England were quickly learned and sung in the colonies. This devotion to all things English included the way to raise children.

In the 1700s, colonial parents followed the child-raising theories of a famous English thinker named John Locke. His book, *Thoughts on Education,* was found in town libraries and private homes everywhere. Today, there are many books that tell parents how to raise children. Back then, there was only one—John Locke's. Parents followed its advice carefully.

When John Locke said that children should learn to dance and swim, and that they should spend time outdoors, colonial children were taught to dance and swim. And, of course, they were sent outdoors regularly. Abigail, her sisters, her brother, and her cousins were all raised according to Locke's advice.

John Locke also wrote about the proper way to educate children. He said that a moral and happy life was built on learning. Abigail's father agreed completely with Locke. Mr. Smith had another reason for wanting his children to be well-educated: It was an important part of the teachings of his church. To be an accepted member of the Congregational Church, people had to be able to read the Bible and sign their names.

Abigail quickly picked up her father's love of learning. Mr. Smith owned a fine library and encouraged his children to use it. He taught Abigail to read from his books when she was very young. There were no textbooks in the Smith house. In fact, in those days textbooks did not exist. Instead, Reverend Smith used the plays of Shakespeare, the poems of John Milton, and translations of Greek and Roman classics to educate his children.

Every day, the family gathered in the library for the day's lesson. Each child took turns reading from a book. Then they discussed the meaning of what they had read. Of all the children, Nabby was the best student. She loved stories and plays. She also enjoyed reading history books and learning about the different countries and peoples of the world.

There was no subject that bored little Nabby. She read as much as she could, as often as she could. The grown-up Abigail Adams was considered one of the best-read women of her time. Even so, she had three regrets about her education. Abigail was a poor speller. Her handwriting was far from perfect. And she never learned to read Greek and Latin.

These skills were taught only in boys' schools. In eighteenth century New England, little girls learned to read English, write their names, do simple arithmetic, cook and sew, and keep house. Rich girls were also taught to play a musical instrument and to behave properly in company. Abigail learned everything that girls were expected to know. But she was never satisfied—there was always more to learn.

Abigail's curiosity about everything made her an ideal companion for John Adams. It also made her a brilliant, well-informed person. When John was an American ambassador to France, and then to England, Abigail impressed the French and English intellectuals. And when he served as the first vice president of the United States and the second president, Abigail Adams earned the respect and admiration of the American people.

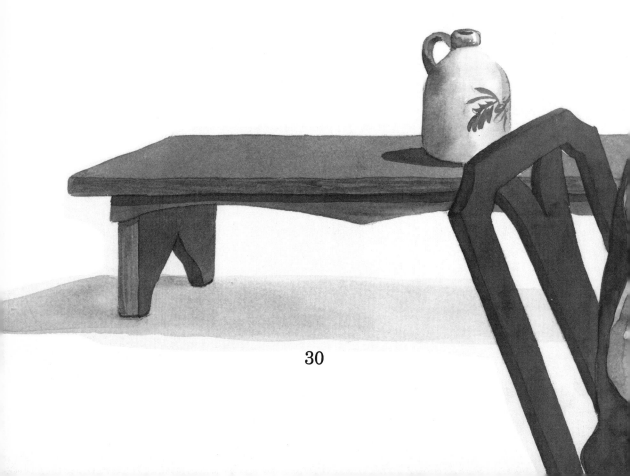

Abigail always enjoyed meeting people. From childhood on, she learned the wisdom of being tactful. She made it a point never to repeat gossip. Instead, she talked about things of interest. Most of all, she was a good listener. After spending time in Abigail's company, people often praised her charming conversation. They seldom realized that they had done most of the talking themselves. In this way, Abigail gained many friends and learned much.

In all her life, Abigail Smith Adams never attended school. Her education in books and real life took place at home, at her grandparents' house, and in Boston. When Abigail was a child, it was common for family visits to relatives' homes to last many weeks at a time. There was no television, radio, or movies then. Travel was difficult, especially in the winter. So people looked forward to having house guests for a month or two. They shared talk, games, and meals. Guests brought variety and change to a house.

33

Abigail Smith loved visiting Grandmother and Grandfather Quincy, her mother's parents. They lived at Mount Wollaston, their estate in Braintree, Massachusetts. It was a large house on a hill, with a beautiful view of the Atlantic Ocean. When Abigail stayed at Mount Wollaston, she and Grandmother Quincy took long walks along the rocky shore. As they walked, they talked.

Abigail had unusual ideas about many things.
This upset Abigail's mother, but not her grandmother. Mrs. Quincy was delighted by the girl's
quick, inventive mind. As Grandmother Quincy
liked to say, "Wild colts make the best horses."

In many ways, Abigail was the sum of her family's teachings. Papa gave her a love of books and ideas. Mama taught her the practical skills of living. Grandmother Quincy gave her faith in herself and encouraged her independent ways.

Another important influence in shaping Abigail was the time she spent in the city of Boston. There she paid long visits to the home of her aunt and uncle, Elizabeth and Isaac Smith. Mr. Smith was a successful merchant. Mrs. Smith was a clever, well-informed woman.

Conversations were lively in the Smith house. The family and their friends talked about everything imaginable: politics, philosophy, science, trade, literature. Abigail listened closely and remembered much of what she heard.

Boston was a bustling city filled with people from all over the world. Abigail heard many different languages there. She tasted many new foods. She enjoyed the busyness of the city—the noise, the variety of people, the mixture of rich and poor, old and new.

In Boston, there was always something exciting to do. Evenings were spent at concerts, lectures, plays, and parties. By the time Abigail was a teenager, the city had helped turn her into a charming, knowledgeable young lady.

Boston's finest gift to Abigail was friendship with people her own age. That was something she really needed. Except for her sisters and brother, Abigail had no young companions back home or at Mount Wollaston.

Of course, there were other young people living in Weymouth. But Reverend Smith's children were not allowed to play with them. It was an unwritten rule that the minister had to be serious and dignified at all times. This was also expected of his wife and children. So the only time Abigail could be a normal youngster was when she was away from home.

In Boston, Abigail became especially close friends with five other girls, Hannah Storer, Eunice Paine, Mary Nicholson, Polly Palmer, and Mary Smith. The six of them remained dear friends throughout their lives. They could not always spend time together, but they always kept in touch by letters.

Abigail also wrote to another dear friend—John Adams. When Abigail first met John in 1759, she was only fifteen years old, and John was twenty-four. Two years later, they met again. This time, John found Abigail more grown up.

The romance of Abigail and John Adams began because of John's friend, Richard Cranch. Richard was in love with Abigail's older sister, Mary. But Richard was shy, so he asked John to go with him to Reverend Smith's home. John, who wasn't shy at all, enjoyed talking about many subjects. So did Abigail. It wasn't long before they found each other's company quite pleasing. And not long after that they fell in love and became engaged to be married.

Abigail and John saw each other as often as possible. But his law practice and her family duties sometimes kept them apart. So they wrote many love letters to each other. In one letter John called her "Miss Adorable" and wrote that he dreamed of her and missed her very much. Abigail called him "Dearest Friend" and wrote that she longed for their wedding day and the beginning of their life together. Finally, on October 25, 1764, Abigail and John were married by Abigail's father.

The habit of letter-writing, which Abigail began as a teenager, became an important part of her adult life. When John Adams was away for long periods of time, as he was during the American Revolution, Abigail and he exchanged many letters. These letters and Abigail's correspondence with her many friends tell us a great deal about the life and times of America in the early years of its history.

Abigail wrote often to John of how she missed him. She described the problems she had in raising the children and running the farm all alone, as well as conditions in New England. She wrote to friends about the books she read, and of her fears and hopes for John and the new nation fighting for its future. And in her later years she wrote a steady stream of letters to her children, grandchildren, and friends. She reported on her life in London, Paris, Washington, D.C., Philadelphia, and everywhere else she and John traveled.

Many years later, Abigail and John's son, John
Quincy, became the nation's sixth president.
Abigail is the only woman who was both the wife
and the mother of U.S. presidents.

Abigail Adams lived a full life. When she died at the age of seventy-three, on October 28, 1818, John Adams wept. They had been married fifty-four happy years. America mourned her passing with him. Her strength, honesty, intelligence, independence, and nobility of mind placed Abigail Adams among the great Americans of her time.

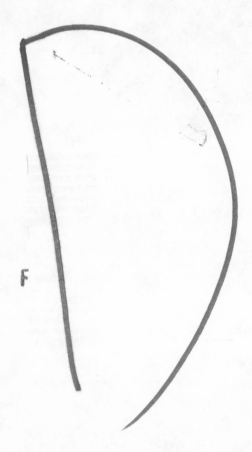

F